changehouse

poems by

michael tregebov

ISBN 0-88801-001-x

Acknowledgements:

Some of these poems have appeared or will appear in the following periodicals: *CVII, Northern Light, Quarry* and *The Winnipeg Centennial Poetry Collection.*

Michael Tregebov was born in Winnipeg on October 31, 1954 of Russo-Rumanian ancestry. He is a student and an avid reader of Marx, Walter Benjamin and Bertolt Brecht. At the present time he is working on a novel.

The poems in this collection were written between 1974-76. The author wishes to thank the editors of Turnstone Press, especially Dennis Cooley and Robert Enright, for their suggestions and advice.

Contents

Dedication:

For Reva, Sara and Gayle
the three generations of women
and all their sisters

Forest Fire

The forest is true to its trees
The lake does not lie to its ripples
But I am an exile from my body.

Fire hangs heavy on the leaves
The lake is a volcano.

The canker's stringbridge of silk;
The spider's fishnet;
Sizzle and go.

Today I've been scared stiff
My two legs are still running.
My breath is in the trees
My love is in the lake.

'There's nothing you can do about it!'
Where was it I was going to?
The lightning squeezed off
A couple of shots.
The rain is smoking everything up.
'It would be better
To have no life than this.'

"It was all only for burning."
As if an otter plunged.
Windy day that was
I stood shaky on my legs
Soaping my wife in the shower
A Japanese mist papers the sky
Deer emerge like water-monsters
The sound sleep is all gone
The words are true to the song.

Cleo

Sitting in the Mozart café
My hand in the trough
The sky is coffee clouded
And my sister Cleo
is all alone.
She is winter.

And with the old words
I write down my regrets
For chucking her out.
Her eyes were blue as whales
Her knees were red and sore
And she rubbed them with embrocation
My sister Cleo
She's not my sister
She's the snow.

I'm unable to be alone
I massage my knees
They were gathering firewood and mushrooms
When I chucked her out
Another day Cleo
And it will swing your way
And I will sponge your knees
For you've ruined them
Burning leaves in the gutter.

My knees are not mine
They're Cleo's
My hands are not mine
They are Cleo's
In the summer they get tanned
They roll a cigarette
They pick, they pinch
but they are not mine.

She could eat five fingers of salami
with one gulp
She sweated like a sausage
And it hurt me that she knew
I was embarrassed for her.

I arrive in my car
I leave on foot
The cold is only a rainbow of steel
Over my house.

She had a tongue of smoked meat
Mine was a slice of onion
Another night Cleo
I see you on a bridge
Two boats pass underneath
The boatmen wave to each other
But not to stranger Cleo,
Because she doesn't have a boat.

Cleo never said goodnight
She said "Ciao"
Down a dark street
The motorcycles scooting
The flickering lights
Two sea cadets walking

My sister Cleo
lying on a dark bed
Pulling on her beard
And probably not thinking of me.

Another night Cleo
And it will swing your way
And I will sponge your knees
Because being alone makes me old
You may be the winter
But I am the cold.

Langside Lip

The melting snow is soaken linen
The highrise grinds into the ground
My hate for winter is regretful now
I sit still as a spot on the floor.
The Assiniboine's surface is green apple
The icefloes hutch like rabbits against the bridge
Branches quarrel with gusto
The wind is an oily shamois
I remain seated.
Wind thunders through the weeds
Melting dung is iron deposit
Copper seam and golden apple.
My fingers are meat cleavers
I crack open the window
I lift up the blue sky
And crawl underneath.

Illuminations

Mongrels are poking their noses
in the puddles of an abandoned gas station

Drinking, raising their wet bearded chins to bark
Pretending to be cars

Winnipeg Beach drowsily washes its face in Lake Winnipeg
Then sits down to a breakfast of washed-up perch

outside our cottage the puddles steam
in the morning sun

illuminations in the cracks and broken glass
collect in clots of ink

I rush to my raft of barrels and boards
Night has moored it on smooth white stones

I push off; into the lake
Poling in the sandy clay

I've grown listless by the lake, my face has
stretched over the cobalt pool

I've grown brown by the lake,
ripples of sand open like venetian blinds
and I stretch to the snows in the north

the arctic landscape illuminated by a
six-month sunset

glowing like a yellow tulip under my eye

I contract like a muscle, back to my boat
bobbing like a buoy, shy, kinetic as a blue-jay

cooling in the water

waiting, listening for my mother's yell of lunch
listening to the creaking poplars, the barking dogs

waves take a long run up, skittering to the shore
flapping like gulls

the lake is ready for take-off
but decides against it

Listening for my mother's voice, her coffeed breath,
The teachers told her: "He's obedient,
But not very well-behaved."

It grows suddenly dark
But now I am floating endlessly, waiting, listening
spying through the black holes of my ship

I hear the ceaseless barking of night
I feel the city lights blowing through the waves

Barking reaches my ears, the city is on fire
the people are destroying the useful things

and dreaming what is possible, igniting numbness
pointing to fingers of fire in the clouds

I strain to hear my mother's call, I think of the cottage
and the barking dogs I'm not allowed to own

the timbers of my raft creak lazily
in exile from the burning city

My head is melting into timber
like chocolate into nuts

The lake enjoys cooling my finger tips,
It drags them through the waves like ten tiny paddles

I wish I could live with handfuls of light
the flash of broken wrists in my eyes forever

I feel sorry for myself, because
I can't make up my mind

Should I stay on my boat
Or float back to shore

I dip my chin in the water
The lake resounds with applause

I raise my eyes: the horizon falls like a curtain, then
The barking dogs: I could pour them in my ears.

Puberty

Across the lake at night
Grand Beach gleams like a watch

My eyes flash and flare like an iguana
My teeth pour out from both sides

The campfire is a crackling corridor
My teeth are charcoal poplars

After sunset there is a steep lawn
Then a copper beach.

Behind the steep lawn is a highrise
The balconies are all pulled out
Like the drawers of a giant dresser.

Behind my back are tangled beeches
My sex is a puma braided in the branches

I am near now
I am there then

Am I part of the present, or a whole of the past
The pike are jumping, I'm a nest in the mast.

In the Sun

In the sun the lake gleams like an eye
At night the tide is its lid closing over.
Fishfly of August
Damp snow of October
The white of green apple
Is soon copper wire
Inches of rich soil
Flame golden sandy tomorrow.
You told me to get out
And I feel sorry for myself
Because you don't know
How middleclass
revenge on me is.
Fishfly of August
Damp snow of October
Kids stealing crabs
Vines drifting through gardens
Spring packs icefloes in the lake
The way *baba* puts her teeth in her glass
And father stuccos with a patch of moonlight
And I feel sorry for myself
Because he knows
what a bargain he's getting.
Fishfly of August
Damp snow of October
The white of green apple
Is soon copper wire.
The smell of August
And the color of my love
fly home together
Fishfly of August
Damp snow of October
The white of my eye
Makes the noise of a flower.
My mother-in-law is a cat
She lifts her leg
And sprays the walls with Florient
Her house is a dark jungle
Full of stuffed badgers
Wallpapered with mirrors
"Nouveau Riche" she calls it proudly.
It brought winter on our heads
My cup is a baritone
It is winter turned over
And what a bugger
Of a winter it was
Because you kicked me out.
Fishfly of August
Damp snow of October
I live in my body
At times it slips away
And my exile then controls me
And I feel sorry for myself
The sky turns black
The horizon zippered in its sleeping bag
The stars are out carving
The moon is hunger
Fishfly of August drinks the snow of October.

12

Wrestling

Don't touch me!
You're all sticky,
everything is sticky
the boardwalk smeared with jelly,
her hair, my palms
the bowl of minnows
the cuffs of her jeans
the pins of the dredger,
windows, hulls, the nails in the dock,
the worms in the leaves,
my spit on the waves,
everything is hot and sticky.
I want to wash, the way I was taught
She wanted to wrestle
But I knew kids weren't supposed to
she grips my neck
her wrists are sugary
her knees pointy
the sun is burning my face
bird feathers stick to my clothes
her fingers dig deep furrows
her voice is vaseline
in my ear
the boat house
ejects its private dock
like a bratty tongue
the bloated perch are beached
the board-deck is tacky
with fresh yellow paint
her arms are machines
screaming in their joints
I resemble her
yellowed papers fly through the streets
the streets are boiling
the sky is sticky with blue the color
everything is the same
life is routine at ten years old
the lake is eating gulls
bloated perch gasp for air
clapping their gills
everything is sticking:
the sands to each other
the sea wall, milk bottles and cream.
worms of asphalt
criss-cross the street,
heat mirages rise
and blur into the horizon
the lake is eating gulls
I want to wash
because I am doing a filthy thing
feathers stick to my clothes
she tears them off
like tufts of candy floss
"I'm uncomfortable
I want to go home!"
But she only grips me tighter
seed tufts are sailing
over a lush field

everything is sticky!
deep furrows dug in gumbo;
the corn; the sunflowers;
the rakes and cattle;
the lips of the beach;
the water tower, and then
a carpet of fishflies
wall to wall on the road to port
and this resort
is a giant melting jelly
smoothing over
a vast poverty and depression.
I want to wash this stickiness away:
from the street signs;
the swinging gates;
the gar grilles; the pagoda; and
the chip shops;
from the eaves and roofs;
from the udders under cows;
I wish I could sponge
you down, down, you
filthy fishy town.
Her fingers dig deep furrows
as we wrestle on the pier
the lake sparkles
I'm full-nelsoned
She's full-nelsoning me
my bones crunch,
the dredge laughs,
the anguished spirits
of the delapidated buildings
sigh with disapproval
The lake is eating gulls
We roll and rock
And fall into the lagoon
her bones were really thin
hollow as flutes
inside I heard whispers
running up and down
in a roller-coaster car
her grip melts from my neck
Cool silence invades
We see devoured gulls,
reds of sea stone,
a giant quarry chiseled out
by the laughing dredger,
our clothes are tattered like crayons
blue germs were forming on the animals
(they know the secrets of the deep).
If only I knew then
What I know now.
Down we come,
Among the chains, the broken blades
of propellers and knives
hook and tackle,
icebergs of arrow heads,
centuries of clay crockery
left by refugee aborigines
Down to the lake-bed
where abandoned dreams
are dumped.

The Changehouse

My father is a shy man
And he holds me by his hand
And we change our bathing suits
At the bath-house by the beach
His old '59 Ford is parked outside
It is a spot on the hill
And the changehouse is muggy
It is a Roman temple
And the echoes are carved in the wall
Along with easy lays
And good blow-jobs
And the humid echoes bounce
With the slap of wet suits
On the concrete benches
And here the men ask:
"What is it that women need?"
And my father being a shy man
Slaps my fingernails
From between my teeth
Outside it grows dark
And from across the lake
Dots and dashes and points of light
Duplicate this changinghouse
And the slap of wet suits
Boom and bang as if to say
This held my balls
But my father is a shy man
And he always folded his suit
Like a sack of flax
And the dirt under his fingernails
Was always gone after a swimming day
And my ears were always oil drums
I emptied them with a slug at my temples
His hair was full of sand
It hung like an old drifting fence
His eyes were green meadows
That were farms once
But I never formed an opinion
Because he was a shy man
And I only saw his dink
In the changehouse by the sand
His legs were scratchy rubble
Fresh mown by work
His cheeks were only soft lines
His back a cord of Chinese snow-peas
And I can see I got my shyness from him.
And he told the strangers
"This is my kid"
Only if they asked
For my father was a very shy man.

He always thought hard and deep
His mind boomed and banged
And I still think dialectics
Are echoes plastering wet frescoes
His teeth are the grille of a '59 Ford
They shine in the archaeological moonlight
And dressed as we are
We shuffle onto the beach
My father was the sunset
And all the wisdom that portends
Yet he never pissed in the sand with me.
He led me by his hand
Up to the edge of the copper shore
Where he dipped his hand down
And lifted the lake
Like the lid of a toy box
He would have given me everything.

For Gayle

When I step out, this balcony is like
The first ring of Saturn:
Still, in night's dimness.
Fiery tongs of flak from a comet
Plunge through the sky
And stagger like drunk pigeons
on the iron rail.

So, to startle you,
Loosened tenderly, like flowing hair
Your laughter breaks like fruit
And sifts each indrawn breath.

And if I let all this loose
For more than music, or fame,
It would be like the orchard;
Daily emptied by the workers there.

1919

The younger I was
The more I lied.
But as I get older I get honester and honester.
The way you thought you knew me
Is not the way I thought you knew me
Your arms fold like windows
Onto the summer lawns.

A hotter summer still was 1919
The water ran out
The green lawns turned yellow
The temperature was rising
The workers were rising
The bread ran out; ran out
The memory of it is coming home.

The earlier I wake
The crankier I get
Waking was a nightmare in 1919
The workers rose too early
To meet their destiny.
Waking was a nightmare in 1919
Dreaming, I slept right through.

I dreamed I was my ancestor
The heat of May lightly falling
I was a six-foot woman
My shoulders were broader than armour
And I was in no hurry to understand.
I was an immigrant ducking the pouring dark
When I spoke in English I drew my ribs tight
I sat on my uncle's porch
I munched on plums
I protested in the park
And felt myself slowly turning grey.
I'm in a photograph of Main Street
History was concrete
With three shallow bullet marks
The streetcar knocked over on its back
Like a beetle kicking in the air
The glass tinkles down the street.
The people were all interesting
But time ran out
Our energy thrashed, ploughed itself under
I was too young, a trouble-maker
I had no need for British lace
The soldiers came in forest green
Spiders laced their boots with webs
Men the size of conifers
But they never passed my armoured shoulders
Framed on my lips, the words:
Wake up! comrade descendant!
When I awoke I was her grandson
I was born before winter
Working things out in advance
And missing the mark.
I embroidered my pillow
For my couch of snow.

Again I dreamed I was my grandmother
I am she who crossed the Atlantic in 1913
I work in a candy factory and wonder
How can anyone be so miserable
Surrounded by all this candy?
I work piece-work, piece by piece
A bend in my back, my eye to the table grain.
I'm a duck midstream in history's pond
I dip my head
My mind clinks of weights and measures —
When I raised my head it was 1919
Seed tufts floated
The sky was drenched blue
Nobody move: Everyone on strike!
Best of all were the meetings in the park
To our right the forest wall
Behind the row of trees the sun shone
Clear and bright as a jewel
Straight ahead the rushing river
Overhanging willow boughs
Shaking their painted curls
Yearning to dip in the river's sex
General Strike: *the hydra head of Revolution!*

I am not an immigrant, only young
Can I come in from the drenching daylight
Without being crushed by you people?
I'll warn you though
I love to be liked.
I'm a sound sleeper
I sleep like a birchwood switch
Nothing bothers me:
Something like that broken tree
Leaning like a broom against the stove.

The Hug

Last night I walked up to the tracks
The train passed with the moon on a flatcar
I've never seen it leave that way before.

Anticipating spring I walked back to the city
Every buzzing street lamp
Asked to fall into my hand
I'm up to my chin in mist
And on my wrist
I lugged my gleaming watch
It was the moon I had lost.

Welders are hovering over stiff street lamps
Sparks come over me like a shower of shooting stars.

My eye is a knot in a tree
My tongue is a slice of onion
Give me a big hug, I'm waiting.

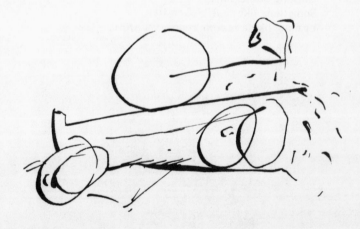

Walking in the City

A low moon is honey in a black spoon
The poor suck on it. Get puffy lips from it.

Don't try to whirl your lips
Pain pierces my body like a pin.

Nerves flash around your head like red lightning
The little kids splash us and take off.

The slush is an amber flood into which I squint
The reflection is a persian blind.

The moon like a honey jar
Pours through the streets.

Walking through the city
I resemble you.

My feet stick, you press on
drag my body like a hockey stick

If I was a woman we'd be good friends
You splash and bring up my past.

You've soaked me
You stupid fool!

"You deserve it, next time pay attention
Don't get carried away with your lies!"

Just before seven the sunset is a liver
It bleeds through the street like a river.

Rough Draft of a Lyric Love Poem from a Woman to a Man

If, in the warmth of your car we ride
And there is a rumbling underneath
You still look at the lovely girls.
My face squirms, my eyes rise in scorn.

The sleet comes down in sheets of foolscap
The grey puddles are dead eyes of the sky.

This winter grayness will soon be over
Confidentially, you share it with me.
Who needs that, who needs you.
Stop the car and let me out.

I walk back downtown and stop at a vending machine
Here I can see my reflection once again
I make my choice of chocolate chunks
I choose the smoothest and milkiest
For two dimes I get a gold package
For two dimes I get to hear the machine
For two dimes I make O Henry happy
For two dimes I make Cadbury jealous
For two dimes I take my country far
For two dimes I even get a chocolate bar.

My hair grows longer every minute
My skin gets dirty no matter how hard I wash
My grandmother has bought her cemetery plot
But she's still in no hurry.

I catch the sunset bus South
The sun is burning in the sky now
The old clouds are strands of red hair
They flow through the streets too.

The sun is extinguished like a cigarette
The puddles dry like cod
They flap their fins under the bus
The transmission plunks on the ground.
The bus driver scratches his head.

I walk the rest of the way home
The houses are swollen vertebrae
The street is a bad back
The moon comes out like a rusty bolt
A stretch of cloud screws it to the black sky.
My hair grows longer than ever.

Conversation with a Chilean Exile

In the winter the trees haven't grown an inch
I've just been digging-in here all my life;
Crawling under this rock called Canada.

Though the window of the sun was grey jelly
I swallowed a lot of saliva
The conversation was an airplane wreck
When we hit upon one topic:
All teachers who have died
Too many reluctant heroes.

Looking at his crowned teeth
Listening to a folk-song
After eating and dancing and talking
I explain: it's not that love's so sad here
It's just that everyone sees it that way.

There is a louse on my collar
Our culture collects in pools
Cars are moving razor blades
The workers only carry capguns
And the university is a crumpled sheet of paper
Until you return I'll still be here.

Asleep in an Upstairs Room
Made Unbearably Hot by August

I'm in the grip of sleep
The street lamps glow
and open the screen doors
of sleeping houses.
I love you
I love your name
It makes me doze
back to sleep.
All the houses are napping;
Electricity zips down the wires
Fluorescent glows Florida
in my dream
The wind calls collect
To Cassalls in Madrid
He strums the telephone strings
They hum between the hydro lines
I turn in my sleep
Like the page of a magazine
My mouth drips loam
I am walking a tightrope
of twined coarse hemp
Because I like the air
up here
Below, the houses
flee through the streets
(Mine takes off without me)
They panic
Like fire in the theatre
They storm the exits
Rushing like refugees
before the borders close
I cast my eyes away from the commotion
I do this tightrope jazz so easily
I could do it in my sleep.
Come down?
Never, not until the last refugee
has a warm bed for sleep,
not until the morning dawn
charges through the window
like horses of butter.

The Week

The lake works hard to give me pleasure
My senses work hard to please me
So on Sunday I went to the beach
All the proletarians were white
They glowed and stuck out.
Which comes first: politics or pleasure?
I took my rubber float
And floated, waited, swept away
To avoid the question.
The little wind made little waves
Like hips of women, hips of men
The sun scattered sparks.

I am taking my beer in Monday's centre
This is the present I have to assume
That I am here as well as the room
A thick cloud leaned its elbow on the house
And down came all the endless rain
Rain everywhere, everywhere rain.

Tuesday I had my goldeye broiled
Took my blue coat to the laundry
This running around makes me weak
On top of it all a load of work
I fought with everyone that day
I'm miserable when the wind's up
And the Seventh Fleet circles
Off the coast of Spain, Portugal, and Italy
Beirut bleeds into the Mediterranean.

Met my old principal on Wednesday
It was like Alaska shaking hands with Siberia
(Across the Bering Strait)
We'd separated such a long time ago
The Americans leaving Africa to make an Atlantic.
I thought of it that night, like
A sail ripping in the harbor,
I thought of it because
My old classmates are too cynical for their age.

By Thursday I realized I was making a week
Because I had an honest talk that day.
Do I know more of you
Or less of your mysteries?
I said: "I'll never stop loving you."
And you believed me.
And when I stopped loving you
You couldn't believe it.
Now you've had lots of time to have lots of men
Some handsomer, some duller, some honester.

If I were an ant I'm sure some kid would say:
"Let this one live, he's not worried about the future."
But it would all be a lie
My friends and I are adversaries
Of Stalin and the bourgeoisie
Revenge is a fever in our pulse,
Like a train
It runs erratic from Auschwitz to Coyocan
Friday's chicken spreads its drumsticks!

When you come right down to it
We share our time but *not* our end.
Saturday stretches like a long horizon
The last rays of the sun's weak slant
The cloud on its haunches smothers me
I crawl underneath the great beast to breathe
Great concerns make great poetry.

Water Lilies

There was a woman who was everything but me.
She lived by the river close to the wind which
Blew every moon-yellow streak through the trees.

September saw me paddling toward the flowered bank
In a blue drama of lilies and things outside me
Composing to the cadence of wind through poplar trees.

The wind blew on one shiny ear and slashed my back
I gestured to the shore, to the prussian clouds
Withering like gardens in the sky.

I'm afraid to cross over to the shore
There the hungry thrush lances the worm
And rings of heat rise before a summer rain.

But the water lilies: pink and red and blue flame;
Pausing and passing like blotted inks;
Heavy as stars deciduous and stars desolate.

The lilies unbind, the winds rage beneath the river
And draw me to her warm brown arms. I dissolve my face
In dew, my mouth fills with water and my eyes behold
The silk worm's bolt of sun unfurled.

Future

Tomorrow, I will wonder
Who are the ones who get anywhere:
The cool-heads under new stars, or
The unanswerable fingers of the musicians.

My eyelids flutter like flowers unfolding,
I wait, sitting on a chair,
My hand folded on one knee,
Feeling the rhythms of knitting.

I am waiting for gloves
Being knit in the room next to me.
When I get them
My fingers will come alive.

My hands will open
And warmth will filter up my wrists,
My arms will feel what is coming:
Lorries of night and weakness.

The Roofer Elegy

Who, if this drunken crowd screamed, would hear us tremble like children.
Tremble beneath the weight of this man's death, like generations of sorrow.
Piled upon our chests, heavy and deep with remorse, and this simple death,
A fall from a roof, a roofer's death, consumed like knotty pine in fire.

His death consumes intricate weavings from the past, a few traces escape the fire:
Like muddy footprints between two rivers in rain; like a bloody fingerprint
Smeared on the page of a detective novel; the silken traces of pine leave behind
Threads and aromas, telling of his life like no marble carving can.

We bury the roofer and smother the man, he bangs on the lid,
He protests, he did not slip from the roof he was patching,
His eye caught sight of a new need, for a moment he stopped
Being a roofer, fell, and began seeing terror that we can stand.

What was it he saw that moment, stretched thin as canvas,
That moment between the players' last line and
The audiences' applause. What force descended upon him that
Separated his soul from his hammer and his foot from the shingles.

This roofer as a child was carried out of the gray forests,
Where he shivered in the arms of a grandmother, crossing
The oceans together they were tossed by the waves and dreams
Of a new world, their faces paled as white as caps on the waves.

His grandmother swam in those waves, and prayed to them,
Saw no ocean but them, and reared the child to be immersed
In the primitive tones they made and hypnotic verse they sang:
trained and targeted in his mind like the constant hammering of hunger.

Beached by these forces, crashing down upon sand, thrown up
By these strange forces from the depths of life and history,
These two characters walk boldly as reason, cunning like
The parable from the Chinese on the tribulations of usefulness:

In the dark forests there are many different kinds of trees:
From the thickest they make timbers for ocean ships;
The thinnest of all are turned to whipping rods and gats.

But from the stunted ones nothing is made at all, these escape
And remain merely trees and that is where the parable ends
And the man begins, walking out of the sea with salt on his lips,
Descending from the forests with fresh lungs of pine wood.

As casual as a glance he lived and then fell from a roof.
He lies apart from us like the stage from the audience
Separated by an abyss, rising from the depths before our eyes,
The abyss which separates living from dead like intoxication.

And the crowd before his coffin sways like a drunken man.
The wind blows through us and the sun shines through
Our bodies while we watch the coffin lowered into the ground,
The tears of his wife rippled in the wind like lakes.

The crowd stares as the grave is filled with earth
They look into the grave and step back slowly, horror-struck
To see the debris piling before their eyes, and like history
Move slowly back, step by step, before running forward.

Brocaded Geese

I pamper my life
The grass is so green
The trees are so lush
There is nothing to look forward to.

The moon is a yellow worm
Look, it has come out too late.
All the others are half-way to cocoon.

Look, the boats are moored
Like brocaded geese
The clouds pillar
The summer rain
Knocks on the trees
In a dirge.
Rain rolls down the window
Like a tea-top.

Civilisation is so young
The universe is in its youth
This is all a sour-yellow plum
Ripening in the rain.

My tongue is a banana peel
Green as a springing bough
I come out of the bath like Balzac
The bronze has turned green
The bedspread is a sheet of lightning.
I open it like an iris.

Leaving Winnipeg

Leaving makes me old
My friends are leaving, leaving.
Out of the house, the house, I go.
I will be leaving the home of my life.
I am leaving the worms to their gumbo
I am leaving the munching cows
Like an old elephant
I make my way to the water
I am leaving behind the skies
That have poured the blue in my eyes
I am leaving for the Pacific
Where all the elephants go to die.
So the family seed, centuries ago,
Started by the walls of Jericho
When one of the trumpeters
And one of the tambourinists
Diddled each other in the clay
Dozens and dozens of dozens of disasters:
Like boys destroying a bee-hive
The Romans tore down the temple
The tribe left for the West
To ancient Europe: Russia and Roumania
Then hundreds of hundreds of troubles
The czarist hooligans
Poked them in the face with pogroms
Then again for the West they left
I can see my grandmother's face
Excited on the dock
The harbour full of snow
She boards the trawler
And across the fat Atlantic goes
Leaving for the city of rail and rivers
I am leaving this frozen cube
I am leaving this land-locked
calendar of the fifties
The river's arms can't hold me back.
In the early autumn
The trees still thick with tangles
Out from the airport station
The heavy plane angles
And from the sky at night
I see below there are space stations
flashing morse code:
Regina in the drowsy arms of wheat;
Calgary a cool basilica of wealth;
Vancouver Island, doing the dead man's float
Lookout, I'm going to jump on your back!

Turnstone Press

Poetry Series
number four

Drawings by Denis Nokony
Designed by Eva Fritsch

Changehouse was printed offset in an edition of 350 copies. Set in Theme 10 point bold. The text is Rolland Tint Ivory; the cover Mayfair Olive and the endpapers are Byronic text apple green.

We gratefully acknowledge a grant from the Manitoba Arts Council that has aided in the publication of this book.

Turnstone Press
St. John's College
University of Manitoba
Winnipeg, Manitoba
R3T 2M5.